Handbook
For
Gay Marriage

(Things to do before saying 'I do')

Written
By
Nigel D. Salmon

Handbook
For
Gay Marriage

(Things to do before saying 'I do')

Handbook For Gay Marriage

ISBN 978-19762-40843
Published 2017

CONTENTS

Introduction

Many individuals enter marriage with expectations of what things should be and not what things are, focusing on what they want to happen and giving less attention to what is happening, or marrying on a self-defined fantasy of marriage rather than the reality of it. The truth is that marriage requires careful consideration before uttering those two simple but life-changing words 'I do."

What is marriage? Whether it happens between heterosexuals or homosexuals, marriage is simply marriage. Marriage cares not if you are gay or straight, Muslim or Christian, black or white, rich or poor. Marriage is, in definition, a union entered by two persons who legally agree to exclusively commit to each other sexually and stick with each other in better or worse, sickness or heath; till death do them apart.

This book is a guide for the males who are in the process to getting married and those thinking seriously about getting married one day. You will be taken through some important considerations for fiancés, few of which you might have overlooked on your own. This book will nudge you to assess yourself, your fiancé, and the status of the relationship between the both of you. Overrall, it is your readiness that this literature puts to the test.

As the title apparently stated, this book is geared toward the gay community. Though all the references point to the male gender, such references include both male and female same-sex couples.

If you do not build your house on the right foundation, it is most likely that the house will fall apart after you have moved into it. Likewise is marriage. If you moved into marriage without first getting the foundation right, the marriage will most likely fall apart. Like bricks or blocks from the falling house that can drop on you and hurt you, marriage when fall apart will hurt someone.

This book is to help you set the foundation for your marriage. You will have to get the foundation right before you can get the marriage right. Foundation is strength.

So what constitute the foundation of a marriage?

You might reply to this question by simply saying 'love.' You would be right, but only partially. It takes more than love. Many people give all the attention to love and the little things they ignore become the nemesis to their marriages. Those 'little things' are the plain reality problems that will not be solved by the emotion called love. For example, your lover constantly squanders his money and you cannot trust him with yours. You both love each other, but love alone will not change that squandering problem that is causing the lack of trust between the both of you. Another example: Your lover is a lapdog to his friends and makes important decisions base on their opinions instead of yours. Sorry, but love will not change this problem.

While you both love each other, you both should deal with the little things that are making one of you uncomfortable before getting married. Love does not solve people's problem. People solve their problems with love.

Apart from love, the foundation for marriage should be built by the right relationship conditions, right partner, right frame of mind, and right time.

Question Yourself

The first step before getting married is to assess yourself. Self assessment is very important. A lot of individuals tend to spend all the pre-marriage period assessing the other person while ignoring self. It takes two to make a marriage work. So don't just ask if the other person is qualified for you, ask if you are qualified for the other person. You must question yourself before even proposing or saying yes to the proposal. Here are few questions to consider:

Do I truly want to live the rest of my life with this person?

This question digs at your own honesty. It would not be judicious in the long term for you to enter marriage being uncertain about life with the other person. You must enter marriage with the certainty that the other person is 'the person' you want to be with for the rest of your life. Don't play with the other person's emotion by having him believe you are doubtless about being his husband. If your mind is at a place where you are not fully sure you want to marry the other person, carefully mull over the thing that is mentally holding you back. Ask yourself whether this thing is really worth hindering you from getting married with a peace of mind.

The thing that is bothering you and making you uncertain about marriage may be pretty much anything.   Maybe you think the other person is too good for you—example, you are addicted to heroin but he does not know. Maybe you are with him mainly as a matter of convenience—example: You have nowhere to live and he is sheltering and financially caring for you, but you are not mentally prepared to enter marriage with him. Or maybe you believe your lover has a fault.

Whatever it is that is bothering your mind about getting married, talk about it with your lover. Be honest. But if you strongly feel that discussing it with your lover will lead to a break up, you may speak to a confidant (even to a counselor anonymously by phone) to get clarity of mind.

Marrying someone you are not certain you want to spend the rest of your life with will most likely cause problem sooner or later.

Am I only superficially attracted to the other person?

In many relationships, love is not based on the right reasons. So it is important to understand the difference between being 'in love' and just being attracted to the other person because of his financial status, physical appearance, or his big penis. You have to understand the difference.

Being 'in love' means you are emotionally attached to who the other person is unconditionally, accepting his human imperfection, while proving your affection by sharing, bearing and caring.   You are attracted to the whole person instead of one or two things about him. From your side, you will treat his mental and physical health as your responsibility, comforting him when he is sad and bathing him if he has a broken arm.

But if you are attracted to the other person because of his appearance, you will most likely leave him if he puts on weight, loses weight, gets physically or facially scared, or starts to wrinkle due to age. If you are attracted to him only because he has lots of money, you will leave him if he goes broke or when you are made financial independent by him. So ask yourself: Are you only in love with one or more superficial things about this person or are you in love to the depth where you are saying "he is my heart and soul?"

Am I getting married because of societal or peer pressure?

Your friends or societal norms might be frequently asking: "Aren't you getting married too?" "You are not getting younger; so what are you waiting on?"

It is understandable that such questions by society or friends can make you feel 'stupid,' or 'left behind' in living your life in the world. But if you are going to get married to satisfy any of these provocative questions, you are not yet ready to tie the knots. You should not get married to 'fit in.' Your marriage will not be lived by society or friends. It will be lived by you.

The Purpose of the Marriage

You must have a clear understanding of why you will get married. Why do you see it necessary to move from being 'boyfriends' to a married couple?

Many gay lovers have jumped into marriage for the wrong reasons. Is your reason right or wrong? Apart from the previously stated considerations, listed below are some **inappropriate reasons** to getting married:

1. <u>Because my lover decides we should:</u>

If you are going to get married only because your lover has decided you both should, it is most likely that you have no bargaining power in the relationship. You might feel powerless to say "I'm not ready for marriage" because your lover is your only support since you were rejected by your own family, friends or even neighbourhood. (Saying no to marrying him would give the feeling that you do not love him).

But marriage must be entered into by two persons who are both mentally ready for it. If you are not mentally ready, you must ask yourself this question: What is hindering me from being mentally prepared to marry this person who is taking care of me? If your answer is:

(a) you don't believe in marriage,

(b) you don't want to be gay for the rest of your life,

(c) you are bisexual and prefer to settle down in marriage with a woman,

(d) your lover takes care of you financially but he is abusive verbally or physically, or

(e) you feel you are too young to enter marriage at this time.

Then you should say no to getting married, respectfully and honestly expressing your reason to your lover. But you must bear in mind that the consequence of this might be a break up of the relationship, because your lover is ready for settling into a marriage—and you are not. It is like two people in a bus and one wants to go left and the other wants to go right. But the bus can only go in one direction.

Have a discussion to come to a compromise if you both really don't want a breakup. The raw reality is to either compromise or separate.

2. <u>Because it is now legalized</u>

The legalization of gay marriage in California, for example, led to many gays rushing into marriage within the first week. Did some of them get married because they wanted to or because they got caught up in the excitement? Don't get drunk because a lot of bear is on the table. In other words, don't get married because you now have the legal right to. Marriage is a legal matter. Calm down, take in a deep breath and reconsider. The fact that you have the legal right to do something does not mean it is right to do it.

3. <u>Because I want my lover to get citizenship</u>

So you have fallen in love with this guy who does not have citizenship status. You feel that the only way to not lose him is to get married so he can get his citizenship. You will do your lover a favour. But will the marriage be in favour of the both of you?

Many marriages for citizenship never last. This is because many individuals desperate for citizenship often feigned romantic love and get married to secure their citizenship status. Once it has been completed, they began showing their true colours.

It would be improper to state that any person who will gain citizenship by reason of marriage will not stay faithful. Many marriages that facilitated citizenship are still happy unions. But the folowing are warning signs that you may look for to avoid getting used by a person who needs his citizenship status and not you:

(a) He wants to get married in days of meeting you,

 (b) He is not interested in knowing much about you except just to marry you.

4. <u>It sounds like a nice thing to do</u>

If you will get married only because 'it sounds like a nice thing to do,' then you are viewing marriage as a fantasy. Your mind is in the wrong place. Marriage is a reality. It becomes part of your reality when you enter it. So don't get married because you feel it sounds like a cool idea. If your lover proposed to you unexpectedly (especially in front a group of people), you may say yes to avoid embarrassing him but should ask for time to consider it through.

Listed below are two <u>appropriate reasons</u> to getting married. These two reasons represent the love that two romantic couples should have for each other. They are:

1. <u>We are ready to settle down</u>

The term 'settle down' used here means that you have made the conscious decision to have no sexual affair other than with the man you will marry. The both of you have to be mentally ready to settle down else the marriage will have problems.

Settling down does not only point to 'having sex only with my partner.' Settle down also includes giving up activities that would come between you and your partner. This means you will have to stop partying out alone, stop entertaining flirting guys, and close down profile you have on any dating website.

2. <u>Security for each other</u>

This is the next suitable and beautiful reason to getting married.   You and your lover are in love and and you want to ensure that should something happen to one of you, such as death, the other is not put at a disadvantage.

Live Together For A While First.

This is a very important action to take prior to marriage. It is important because it allows the both of you to understand more about each other before becoming a legally recognized couple. By living together for a while (a month the least) you both will crasp what the other like and don't like outside of sex.

Irritating habits

You will not know how many of your habits, or how many of your partner's habits, are intolerable until you both experienced living together. Habits that works fine when you are a single man might not work well when you become a husband. This is because as a single guy, you are living for 'me'. But as a husband, you will be living for 'us.'

When you live with your husband-to-be, things you do around the house will affect him. So think about your lover in everything you do around the house. Things that you have gotten accustomed to doing alone might become irritating habits to your lover. You will have to be open to eliminating or altering such habits. Remember that living with your lover creates a shared life, no longer a me-life.

On the next two pages are habits that tend to become bad habits when sharing space with someone else:

Untidy: While living single, leaving clothes on the floor, not spreading the bed, leaving unwashed plates in the sink for a while, not bathing every night before bed, hanging dirty clothes in the bathroom, etc. were not a problem. But when you begin sharing space with your lover, such activities will most likely be seen as—which they are—untidy.

Frequently having friends over in the house: When living single, having friends frequently in the house is understandable company. But now that your husband-to-be is living in the house, your friends (or relatives) should not be frequently in and around the house. A romantic couple needs to have their own private space, especially in their home.

Playing loud music often: This can easily become an irritating habit if you have not eastablished that your husband-to-be enjoys frequent loud music. Loud music is a serious nuisance to many persons. You will know if your fiancé is one of such persons by the experience living together. The compromise should be in favour of the partner who cannot tolerate the loud music. This is because loud music has the capability to harm while low music hurts no one.

Spending too much time online: These days a lot of individuals are spending more time on the internet and less time with the persons physically around them. If you have this habit, it will sooner or later negatively affect your fiancé. Attention is very important in a romantic relationship. Too much time using the internet and not much 'us time' will kill the romance between the two of you. Give attention to your fiancé by give up unnecessary browsing time.

<u>Laziness around the house:</u> If your fiancé tells you that you are not helping much in the house, believe him. It is not a good thing for only one of you to be always doing the dishes, cleaning, clothes washing, groceries, and other household work. Even if you work and your fiancé stays at home, you should assist him when around the house to give him some peace of mind.

<u>Masturbating a lot</u>: Masturbation is really a 'me thing.' If you or your fiancé often goes to the bathroom or some other place of solitude to self pleasure, the other partner might start to feel uncomfortable. Masturbation is arguably a bad habit in marriage. The point here is not that you or your partner should stop masturbate when you begin living together. The point is that it can become a bad habit when you often spend time doing it by yourself.

Decide On Children

This is a very important consideration and a subject of discussion before getting married. If each of you has no child, you must individually decide on whether you both will adopt or each produce biological children before marriage. If one of you has biological children and the other doesn't, the one who is without must state whether or not he has the desire to have biological children.

Recording artiste Ricky Martin first produced two biological children before he came out of the closet and began living a full homosexual life. He did this to ensure that he never had to cheat on his same sex lover. So discuss each other's state of mind on the issue of children before the wedding bell. Do you both wish to adopt, have biological children, or have no children?

It is not a judicious attempt for one of you to try convince the other to adopt instead of having a biological child or vice versa. If you or your fiancé wishes to have a biological child, it would be better to do so before getting married. If you convince him out of having a biological child, he might later suffer from a sense of 'unfulfilment' on the subject of fatherhood and blame you for it. So the fiancé who does not want a biological child should not try to prevent the other from such path. Together the both of you may adopt one or more children.

If both of you decide to adopt children but after
marriage one of you has a change of mind in favour
of having a biological child, there is always the option
of a surrogate mother.

Decide on roles you both will play

Traditions have long established the roles of men and women in heterosexual marriages. For example, by tradition the woman takes care of home duties like clean, wash, cook and look after the children while the husband goes to work. While the same can be applied to a gay marriage, it usually does not occur that way. So it may be necessary to decide on roles the both of you will play in the marriage.

Discussing roles is particularly important if the both of you have not lived together for a reasonable time while the wedding date gets near. In your discussion, cover as many thinngs as you both desire. Regarding sex, who will play top? Regarding home duties, who is in the position to mainly handle this role? Regarding the children (if any), who is in the position to mainly look after them?

Without even thinking of it, though, roles might be naturally established in the relationship. For example, your lover takes care of cleaning the house, wash and cook without any prior decision between the both of you for him to take on such role.

The point is that, if necessary, clarify roles in the relationship before marriage. This may prevent later disagreement between the both of you.

Marriage is a reality, not fantasy

You are excited about your upcoming wedding. You are now envisioning all the wonderful things that you will do as a married couple. Without actually saying it, you are thinking about living 'happily ever after.' You are thinking about how exciting your marriage is going to be. Ok, nothing is wrong with that kind of thinking. It is necessary. But you must bear in mind that marriage is not a fairytale. It is a reality which you and your spouse must live every day.

Problems will come, meaning that your partner will do things that you don't really like. You will also do things your partner does not like. Things physical and facial about your partner will change—example, he starts to moult, you start to gain weight. Circumstances will also change—example, the time you both spend canoodling will reduce as time passes after the marriage.

To deal with the reality of marriage, you both have to give attention to understanding each other's personality, habits, likes and dislikes. You have to listen to each other's opinions but accept that you will not at all times agree with what the other thinks. Respect the feelings of each other and allow compromise in the union. Make it a policy to always discuss things together in order to smoothly solve problems.

Remember, it's not marriage that makes a happy couple. It's the couple that make a happy marriage.

The Wedding Day

Whether your wedding will be a simple ceremony with few guests or a fabulously expensive event with lots of guests, the wedding day is the door to a legal union of life together with the one you love. It is a special day. A wedding can take a lot of preparation—from getting the marriage licence, choosing a conveient day, sending out invitations, budgeting, etc. So below are just few selected things you should do:

Look happy and smile a lot.

When there is only days or hours to go before the wedding, others (relatives, friends, neighbours, co-workers, etc) will be observing your behaviour. Their expectation is to see you exuding happiness. So don't keep your happiness on the inside. You need to let it be seen, especially to your fiancé. When talking to others about the wedding, you should converse with a smile. Smile a lot and look happy.

Choose clothes your partner will like.

Maybe the both of you will go renting or shopping for the outfits you both will wear. In this case, your fiancé will throw in his opinion on what he thinks you should choose. But if you will separeately shop for outfits, ensure as much as possible that you choose something that fits the taste of your husband-to-be in terms of colour and design.   If you are too uncertain about what will please him, just ask him what he would like to see you in.   If he says something like "just choose something nice, baby," then follow your intuition.

Do not make love for at least a week before the marriage.

If you really want to excite the wedding night (the night after getting married), you both should make yourselves hungry for sex with each other. By not have sex with your fiancé for a week or more before marriage, you both will be so thirsty and hungry that you will eat each other up from the moment you walk in through the door as a married couple.

Do not kiss before being pronounced married.

It is not wise to let your guests see the both of you kissing before being pronounced married. Why? Wedding guests typically applaud after the marriage officer pronounces the couple married and asks them to kiss each other. If the guests saw the both of you kissing before, they might not be particularly excited when seeing you kiss as married couple. So don't make the kiss stale by doing it before the given time.

Look in your partner's eyes.

This is a very important instruction to follow especially when standing in front the marriage officer. You must not be looking down or slightly away from your husband-to-be. The both of you are the centre of attention of the guests and they are observing the way you both interact in front them. So whenever you are looking at each other, look directly in the eyes.

Do not invite anyone who do not condone gay marriage.

It is your big day and you probably want to invite persons important in your life. But if your parents, for example, are not comfortable about you marrying someone of the same sex, then you should not invite them. Numerous times weddings have been disrupted by individuals who had some kind of objection. By law an individual may object to two persons getting married. The marriage officer must make room for anyone to object by saying the following: *"If anyone can show just cause why this couple should not be joined, let that person speak now or forever hold their peace."* This provision for objection is to really protect the marriage officer from carrying out a marriage that would be in breach of the law. A person objecting must prove that the marriage would be in breach of a law. Subjective objection is useless and can only cause commotion. But a commotion can be embarrassing. So if you know someone is already objecting to your homosexual lifestyle base on personal or religious reason, do not invite such person.

Say your own wedding vow

Marriage officers are given the pre-written vow that they will ask the couple to repeat. The important thing is that the couple, or one of them, can replace it with his own written or ad lib vow. Saying your own vow is hereby recommended as   it allows you to express your deepest emotion   to the man you are marrying.

Your own vow puts you in that moment, before the eyes of all those present, to say how your husband-to-be made you felt when you first met him, how he is affecting your life for the better, and how you promise to be truthful, kind and be the man of his life as long as you live.

End

About The Author

Nigel D. Salmon is an author, songwriter, entrepreneur and the founder of Life Support Jamaica. He loves to read and meet new people who share his interests. He lives in St Elizabeth, Jamaica.

Website: www.NigeldSalmon.com

Facebook: Nigel D. Salmon

Instagram: Nigel D. Salmon

Twitter: Nigel D. Salmon